Maths Together

There's a lot more to maths than numbers and sums;
it's an important language which helps us describe, explore and
explain the world we live in. So the earlier children develop
an appreciation and understanding of maths, the better.

We use maths all the time – when we shop or travel from one
place to another, for example. Even when we fill the kettle we are
estimating and judging quantities. Many games and puzzles
involve maths. So too do stories and poems, often
in an imaginative and interesting way.

Maths Together is a collection of high-quality picture
books designed to introduce children, simply and enjoyably, to
basic mathematical ideas – from counting and measuring to pattern
and probability. By listening to the stories and rhymes, talking about
them and asking questions, children will gain the confidence to
try out the mathematical ideas for themselves – an important
step in their numeracy development.

You don't have to be a mathematician to help your child
learn maths. Just as by reading aloud you play a vital role in
their literacy development, so by sharing the **Maths Together** books
with your child, you will play an important part in developing their
understanding of mathematics. To help you, each book has detailed
notes at the back, explaining the mathematical ideas that it
introduces, with suggestions for further related activities.

With **Maths Together**, you can count on doing the
very best for your child.

For Steve

With thanks to Jeannie Billington and Grace Cook
who collected the games and puzzles, and Carole Skinner
who created the game "Give Away", first
published in *Nursery Games* (BEAM)
as "Ten Lovely Things".

First published 1999 by Walker Books Ltd
87 Vauxhall Walk, London SE11 5HJ

2 4 6 8 10 9 7 5 3 1

© 1999 Nick Sharratt
Introductory and concluding notes
©1999 Jeannie Billington and Grace Cook

This book has been typeset in Sassoon Primary.

Printed in Singapore

British Library Cataloguing in Publication Data
A catalogue record for this book is
available from the British Library.

ISBN 0-7445-6834-X (hb)
ISBN 0-7445-6826-9 (pb)

MOUSE
MOVES HOUSE
Activity Book

Nick Sharratt

WALKER BOOKS

AND SUBSIDIARIES

LONDON • BOSTON • SYDNEY

Matty the mouse is moving house. He's asked Sid and Ruby's removal company to help him. Sid and Ruby arrive with their furniture van.

beep!
beep!

Hi there!
I'm so glad
you've come!

Sid and Ruby's Square Game
(2 players)

You need:
8 counters of the same colour each (or you could use silver and copper coins)

Take it in turns to put a counter on a dot. The first person to cover 4 dots that would make a square if joined up, wins. Some of the squares you can make are not immediately obvious.

Matty hasn't finished packing. He's not sure which things to put in which boxes. Can you help?

Can you find a way to measure Ruby's strings?

6

They load up the van with Matty's furniture. Matty's neighbours are very strange. They're all invisible!
How many people do you think there are in next door's garden?

Everything is in the van and it's time to set off. Can you find a way to get to Matty's new house without crossing any bridges? A bumpy ride might damage his furniture!

They've made it at last! Matty unlocks the door and goes inside.

Odds and Evens
(2 players)

You need:
a dice, a counter each

Decide which player is going to be "odds" and which "evens". Take it in turns to throw the dice. If an odd number is thrown, the "odds" player moves forward; if it's an even number, the "evens" player moves forward. The winner is the first to get past 27.

27 26
23 24 25
18 17 16
13 14 15
8 7 6
3 4 5

Sid and Ruby play RATS! as they unload the furniture.
Why don't you have a game too?

Rats!
(2 players)

Starting from 1, take it in turns to count 1, 2, or 3 numbers at a time. So the first player says "1", "1,2" or "1,2,3" and the second continues. Whoever gets to 20 wins, and the loser shouts "Rats!"

Now we've got to unpack everything!

How many squares can you find in the rug?

What a lot of squares!

Oh dear, there's a mug missing!
Can you work out which one it is?

MUGS		✓
SPOTS	STRIPES	
2	1	
2	2	
4	2	
2	3	
3	2	
1	3	
1	3	

Matty's friends Sadie and Tom call by to see how he's getting on. Moving house can be hard work, but it's easy for Sadie and Tom...

Give Away
(2 players)

You need:
*a dice, 10 little objects each
(buttons, shells, coins, counters etc.)*

Decide which player is going to be
the snail and which the tortoise,
and each put your objects on
your animal. Take it in turns to
throw the dice, say the number
aloud and give the other player that
number of things. If the number
on the dice is more than the number
of things you have left, then you
miss a go. The winner is the first
person to give all their things away.

Life's simple when
you've got a shell!

About this book

Mouse Moves House is designed to develop children's mathematical skills through play. Playing games and solving puzzles are great ways to make them feel at home with numbers, shapes and space. They encourage children to think logically and clearly, and to work out mathematical strategies which they can build on.

Games

Children enjoy games and often want to play them over and over again. They may want to change the rules of the games in this book to make them easier or harder. The answer pages at the back also suggest variations. Playing in teams as well as individually, children learn to listen and observe, to share ideas and to work together.

Sid and Ruby's Square Game develops children's awareness of shape because it encourages them to imagine the squares from unusual viewpoints. Along with the other "dotty" games at the back of the book, it also gives them a chance to use spatial language and strategic skills as they decide where to put their marks.

Packing Boxes helps children think about the space that something takes up (volume) and the amount of space inside something (capacity). **Ruby's String** helps with estimating, comparing, and ordering length.

There are three counting games. In the easiest, **Give Away**, the counting is in ones; **Odds and Evens** is about recognizing numbers and counting on a grid; **Rats!** can be played on many levels – it uses mental maths and may be more difficult than the others at first. Each of these games involves different degrees of luck, fairness and skill: **Give Away** is based purely on chance; **Rats!** needs strategy and skill; **Odds and Evens** is unfair! You can help your child by talking about how each game works (for example, Why is **Odds and Evens** unfair? How could you make it fair?). Children get more confident at making decisions when they understand the kind of game they are playing.

Puzzles

Puzzles are mathematical ideas presented in meaningful situations. They are one of the best and most enjoyable ways of learning mathematics. Like a detective on a case, a child trying to solve a puzzle will often follow a hunch. Even if the hunch turns out to be wrong, it makes them check and test their ideas. You can help by watching and encouraging children to talk things through.

The **Invisible People** and **Spot the Difference** puzzles involve observation. You may find it helpful to keep a note of what you've spotted before looking at the answers.

Finding the Way provides opportunities for developing spatial awareness and introducing simple maps.

Rug Puzzle, in which there are a number of hidden squares, develops children's spatial skills. They may also need to find a way of keeping count.

Matty's Missing Mug is a matching puzzle. By matching the mugs to Matty's list, children will discover which is missing by elimination. They might enjoy designing other mugs with spots and stripes.

Matty's Cushion Puzzle has a mathematical pattern. Children can solve it by trial and error, or by using a systematic approach (as shown in the answer pages). What would happen if there were four cushions?

Upside-down Picture gives you the chance to think about what something might look like when it's turned round.

Notes for parents

Sid and Ruby's Square Game *pages 4 and 5*

Playing this game helps children see how different squares can be made. They can be of different sizes and they can be tilted.

Tracing Dots

Trace these dots on to a piece of paper.
Use 16 dots (4 x 4) to play *Linking, Top to Bottom, Boxes* and *Noughts and Crosses*.
If you use all 64 dots (8 x 8), the first three games will be much harder!

Linking
(2 players)

Take it in turns to draw a straight line across, up, down or diagonally, joining up the dots. Your line can be as long as you like. The first player can start wherever they like, but from then on each player must start from one end of the line. Your line must not cross another line, or close a shape.
The winner is the player who draws the last possible line.

Noughts and Crosses
(2 players)

Draw 4 lines as shown. One player is noughts and one is crosses. Take it in turns to put a 0 or X in each box. The winner is the first person to make a row of 3, up and down, across or diagonally.

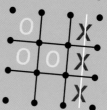

Top to Bottom
(2 players)

Starting at the dot in the bottom left corner, take it in turns to draw a straight line up or across to the right, joining up the dots. Your line can be as long as you like. The winner is the player who lands on the dot in the top right corner.

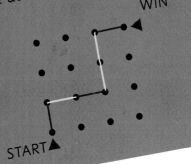

WIN

START

Boxes
(2 players)

Take it in turns to draw a straight line across, up or down joining 2 dots. If you draw the fourth line which closes a square, write your initial in the box and have another turn.
The winner is the person with the most boxes at the end.

25

Ruby's String *page 6*

Together you can discuss how to measure the 3 bits of string.
You could use real string, ribbon or plasticine, or even buttons or small plastic bricks.
Let your child decide.

shortest   longest   middle length

Packing Boxes *page 7*

or

Invisible People *pages 8 and 9*

There are 8 invisible people in the garden:

Finding the Way *pages 10 and 11*

This is the way the van went to Matty's new house, avoiding all the bridges. Now see if you can do the journey crossing *all* the bridges, and then only the *red* ones. Which way is the shortest? Can you also find the shortest way from Matty's house to the library, to the swimming pool and to the swings?

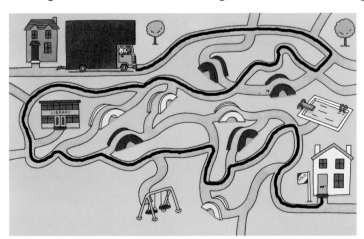

You and your child might enjoy making your own mazes. You can try drawing them, or building them with plastic bricks.

Odds and Evens *pages 12 and 13*

After you've played this game many times, you may realize that it's not fair! The "evens" player is more likely to win because the total of the even numbers on the dice (2 + 4 + 6) is greater than the total of the odd numbers (1 + 3 + 5).

You could also try inventing other games using the coloured squares. For example, take it in turns to throw the dice and move your counter that number of squares. If you land on a red square, go forward 2, if you land on a blue square, go back 1.

Rats! *pages 14 and 15*

Rats! is a wonderful counting game because you can play it anywhere at any time. You will find that the person who gets to 16 can always win.

Example A: 16 | 17 | 18, 19, 20

Example B: 16 | 17, 18 | 19, 20

Example C: 16 | 17, 18, 19 | 20

4, 8 and 12 are also good numbers to land on. Can you work out why? And can you work out why the person who starts is always able to win? Vary the game by only counting 1 or 2 numbers at each go, by playing with more than 2 people, or by counting in even numbers up to 40 (**2**, *4 6 8*, **10 12**, *14* etc.).

Spot the Difference *pages 14 and 15*

There are 7 differences:

1 green door, blue door
2 open door, closed door
3 rectangular window, arched window

4 no round window, round window
5 no curtains, curtains
6 2 chimneys, 1 chimney
7 no aerial, aerial

Matty's Cushion Puzzle *page 16*

There are 6 different ways to arrange the cushions:

Rug Puzzle *page 17*

There are 11 squares in the rug:

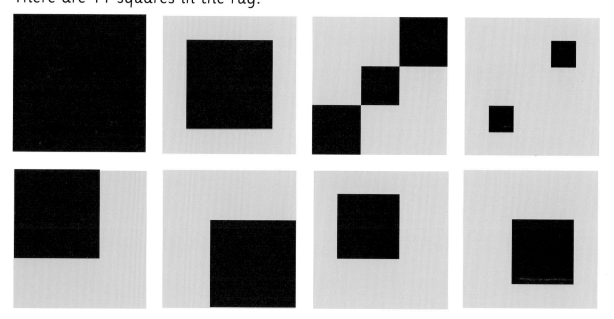

Matty's Missing Mug *page 18*

Oh, look! Here's my missing mug.

MUGS		
SPOTS	STRIPES	
2	1	
4	2	✓
2	2	✓
3	3	✓
1	2	✓
1	3	
		✓

Ask your child useful questions as you play:

Maths Together

The **Maths Together** programme is divided into two sets – yellow (age 3+) and green (age 5+). There are six books in each set, helping children learn maths through story, rhyme, games and puzzles.

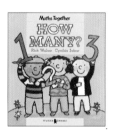

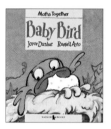

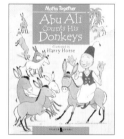